You're

a

Diamond!

Other Books by Krystle

Love Yourself First
How to Heal from Toxic People, Create Healthy Relationships & Become a Confident Woman

Love Yourself First
The Workbook

Self-Love Everyday
31 Empowering Affirmations

Let's Be Honest
Real Answers for Real Women Facing Abuse

After Abuse
(6-Part Series)

Children's Book:

Anna's Dancing Animal Alphabet

When I Think of You

You're a Diamond!

Krystle Laughter

All Scripture quotations, unless otherwise indicated, are taken from the Holy Bible, New International Version®, NIV®. Copyright ©1973, 1978, 1984, 2011 by Biblica, Inc.™ Used by permission of Zondervan. All rights reserved worldwide. www.zondervan.com The "NIV" and "New International Version" are trademarks registered in the United States Patent and Trademark Office by Biblica, Inc.™

"Scripture quotations marked (ESV) are from the ESV® Bible (The Holy Bible, English Standard Version®), copyright © 2001 by Crossway, a publishing ministry of Good News Publishers. Used by permission. All rights reserved."

Scripture quotations are taken from the Holy Bible, New Living Translation, copyright ©1996, 2004, 2007, 2013, 2015 by Tyndale House Foundation. Used by permission of Tyndale House Publishers, Inc., Carol Stream, Illinois 60188. All rights reserved.

Scripture quotations from The Authorized (King James) Version. Rights in the Authorized Version in the United Kingdom are vested in the Crown. Reproduced by permission of the Crown's patentee, Cambridge University Press.

Scripture taken from the New King James Version®. Copyright © 1982 by Thomas Nelson. Used by permission. All rights reserved.

Scripture taken from the Holy Bible: International Standard Version®. Copyright © 1996-forever by The ISV Foundation. ALL RIGHTS RESERVED INTERNATIONALLY. Used by permission.

Scripture quotations marked HCSB are taken from the Holman Christian Standard Bible®, Copyright © 1999, 2000, 2002, 2003, 2009 by Holman Bible Publishers. Used by permission. Holman Christian Standard Bible®, Holman CSB®, and HCSB® are federally registered trademarks of Holman Bible Publishers.

Cover Design by Krystle Laughter

You're a Diamond™
Copyright © 2016 by Krystle Laughter
Tacoma, WA 98409

All rights reserved. No portion of this book may be reproduced in any form without the written permission of the author.

Dedication

This book is dedicated to all the women who never felt good enough or pretty enough. You will never be more perfect & lovely than you are right now. You are a diamond and it's your time to shine!

Thanks

Thank you to all the women who have inspired me and shaped me into the woman that I am today! Your life, example, and encouraging words have made a world of difference in my life.

A special thanks to my mother-in law, Mrs. Sarah Parker and my sister, Nicole Scott for editing this book. Your kind and gentle spirits are a breath of fresh air.

To my mother, who carried me and gave me life. I will always be grateful. Your strength and endurance are inspiring.

To my daughters Sarai, Joelina-Ruth, Joelianna & Hannah. I love you and I thank you for letting me be your mother. I promise to laugh with you and celebrate your life daily. When you feel discouraged I pray you will lean in the arms of the One who created you. You are precious jewels and I will always adore you.

Table of Contents

Day 1: True Beauty..13

Day 2: Cashews..17

Day 3: A Hundred is a Hundred............................21

Day 4: Enough...25

Day 5: Yes, Yes! No, No!....................................29

Day 6: Fear of Success......................................33

Day 7: Blabber Mouth..37

Day 8: Rock Steady...41

Day 9: The Best Dressed....................................45

Day 10: Unshakeable...49

Day 11: From Craze to Praise.............................53

Day 12: Are You Gonna Eat That?.......................57

Day 13: Relax, it's Just a Test............................61

Day 14: Quit Lying...65

Day 15: Grudges Come Easy...............................69

Day 16: Ain't Nobody Got Time for That............73

Day 17: A Fool is as a Fool Does............77

Day 18: Weakness is the Greatest Strength............81

Day 19: Seeing Isn't Believing............85

Day 20: Believe & it Will Come............89

Day 21: Your Gift Will Make Room............93

Day 22: A Wise Tongue............97

Day 23: Wise Time............101

Day 24: What Have You Been Eating?............105

Day 25: All I Need............109

Day 26: Beaches & Bikinis............113

Day 27: Theft............117

Day 28: Flattery............121

Day 29: He is God............125

Day 30: You Got This!............129

Charm is deceptive, and beauty is fleeting; but a woman who fears the LORD is to be praised.
-Psalm 31:30

Day One

True Beauty

People look at the outward appearance, but the LORD looks at the heart.

-1 Samuel 16:7

    Too often, I have been guilty of judging things by their appearances instead of the way God sees them. Samuel, a prophet in the Old Testament, was guilty of this as well. After God rejected Saul from being king, God sent Samuel to go and anoint one of the sons of Jesse. Upon laying his eyes on Jesse's tall and handsome son, Eliab, Samuel thought to himself, "This must be God's chosen one!". But God quickly corrects Samuel and tells him not to consider his appearance because he has already rejected him. In the end, God tells Samuel to anoint Jesse's youngest son, David.

    In a culture that puts so much emphasis on outer appearances, it's easy to judge ourselves and others by the way they look. Most of us have been on both sides of the coin; judging and being judged by others. Yet our loving Father calls us higher. Let us consider the fact that Samuel invited all of Jesse's sons to the feast, yet David's father didn't even think enough of him to invite him. However, David was called by God from tending the sheep to being anointed king of Israel.

People may not consider you or give you a second glance. But our Heavenly Father sees what man overlooks. Hallelujah! Don't allow people to make you feel small or belittle you. You are great in God's sight!

Prayer:

Father, I thank you for seeing me for who I am. I thank you that I am fearfully and wonderfully made. Thank you for counting me in when others have counted me out. Forgive me for any time I have judged others solely by their appearances. Help me to see as You see and love as you love. Amen.

Reflections:

Why is it easy to judge others by outward appearances?

___

___

___

___

How does God judge us?

___

___

___

___

Day Two

Cashews

He heals the brokenhearted and binds up their wounds.
-Psalm 147:3

There was a moment when I realized a truth: *Wholeness has value.* God himself was willing to pay for what He deemed "valuable". I learned this lesson in a grocery store as I wobbled my pregnant frame down the aisle of my favorite health food store seeking to indulge my craving for cashews! For days they were all I could think about; and soon I would be eating them. As my eager eyes slowly scanned the nut-lined shelves, I couldn't help but notice the many types of nuts they had on display. However, the kind that I wanted came with only two choices. One was marked $7.99 and the other $5.99.

Being the bargain shopper that I am, I had to compare the two and discover the reason for the price variation. Were they different sizes? No, they both read sixteen ounces each. They were both raw and unsalted, just the way I liked them. Then, Bam! I caught it. The higher priced cashews were whole cashews, and the cheaper ones were broken pieces of cashews.

"What's the big deal?" I thought to myself, but as I further pondered the situation, I realized that I didn't want broken cashews either. I wanted the whole ones. Why? I'm not sure. Maybe I thought they looked better. Whatever the reason, I paid the extra two dollars for them.

Daughter of God, The King of Heaven, your Father, thought you were important enough for His Son to die for. He wanted to take all of your broken pieces and make you whole again. No matter where you've been or what you've done, you're not beyond the redeeming power of our Precious Savior, Jesus Christ.

Prayer:

Father, thank You for your great love for me. I know that I have done nothing to deserve it. It is Your desire for me to be made completely whole. I ask that You heal me of all brokenness. I want to be the perfect image of Your grace. Heal me and make me whole, in Jesus' name. Amen.

Reflections:

Why does God want you to be whole?

_____

_____

_____

How will your wholeness benefit you or others?

_____

_____

_____

How does God make us whole?

_____

_____

_____

Day Three

A Hundred is a Hundred

Are not two sparrows sold for a penny? Yet not one of them will fall to the ground outside your Father's care. And even the very hairs of your head are all numbered. So don't be afraid; you are worth more than many sparrows.
-Matthew 10:29-32

  A well known pastor held a crisp one-hundred dollar bill in his hand and asked his congregation who wanted it. As you can imagine, a slew of hands flew up all around the building. The pastor then went on to ask his followers if they would still want the hundred dollar bill if it were drenched in mud or stuck in a pile of garbage. Still hands all around the building remained lifted. Why would anyone want a dirty, stinky, wadded up bill? The wise pastor allowed one of his own to answer the question: "Because that doesn't change its value," the man gleamingly stated as he approached the podium. Not only was the man correct, but he also left one-hundred dollars richer that night.

  So, it is with God's precious daughters. The world soon tells you that you're less valuable because you don't fit it's unrealistic standards. The world itself doesn't even live up to them. Those paper-thin models and celebrities we adore are often photoshopped beyond recognition.

If you were to see them without their makeup and accessories, you might not recognize them.

Beloved, God created you perfectly. No amount of makeup, surgery, or weight loss could ever make you more valuable than you are right now! You are His diamond; so don't let anyone stop your shine!

Prayer:

Father, let me see the beauty that you have given me. Forgive me for basing my worth on my outward appearance. Allow me not to be moved by unrealistic beauty standards. Help me to accept myself and love myself just as I am. Help me to change the areas I am not satisfied with in a healthy way and for the right reasons. Amen.

Reflections:

What is beauty?

_____

_____

_____

_____

How does the portrayal of beauty by Hollywood affect you?

_____

_____

_____

_____

Day Four

Enough

Keep your life free from love of money, and be content with what you have, for he has said, "I will never leave you nor forsake you.
-Hebrews 13:5 (ESV)

You see it everywhere, from your favorite t.v. show to your favorite fashion magazine: the pull, the lure to get more, to want more, and to have more. According to an old saying, "You can never have too much of a good thing." But is this true? If we're not careful, we can allow the subtle discontentment of wanting "more" to get the better of us. It usually happens so discretely that we barely notice it. Overtime we become less thankful, begin to complain, and can even blame God for not giving us what we want.

Truthfully, daughter of God, I myself have been guilty of this on many occasions. As a wife, mother, recording artist and author I have found it easy to become 'burned out' to the point of wanting it all to be about me. After all, I deserve it, right?

God created us to want more, but the more we should be seeking is more of Him, His presence, and His grace and love in our daily lives.

Prayer:

Father, give me a heart that longs for you. Take away every selfish desire to want everything I see just because others have it. Let me not measure my worth by the abundance of things, but by your gracious love towards me. Amen.

Reflections:

How has the pull for more affected you and your family?

_____

_____

_____

What can you do to prevent discontentment from taking root in your heart?

_____

_____

_____

_____

_____

Day Five

Yes, Yes! No, No!

...But let your "Yes" be "Yes," and your "No," "No," lest you fall into judgment.
-James 5:12 (NKJV)

Have you ever been in a restaurant with someone who couldn't make up his mind about what to order, or in a drive through as your friend changes her order for the fifth time? Your stomach roars as they go back and forth over whether they want chicken or beef. "Come on! Is it really that serious?" you think to yourself. I must say that I have been guilty of this myself. What is it about having so many options that leaves us unable to make a decision?

Why does the Word of God clearly tell us to be concrete in our response? I know, for me, there have been many times I have waivered telling a friend or even my children, "...we'll see", or "if there's time later we'll do such and such"; only to forget about it or neglect to get around to it. God has wisdom that we don't have; and He knows our hearts. If our hearts are truly attached to something, we will make time for it. As the saying goes, "People make time for the things they want to do."

When we make wavering statements such as, "maybe" or "ask me later", there leaves room for disappointment and hurt on the part of those to whom we speak. If we're not sure whether we can commit to something, our answer should be "no" until we can.

Prayer:

Father, Your word says to let my yes be yes and my no be no. Please forgive me for the times I have waivered and disappointed those in the process. You said if I ask without doubting, You would give me wisdom from heaven. I ask that You give me wisdom from above, the courage to say no when I should, and the integrity to follow through on my commitments. In Jesus' name, Amen.

Reflections:

Why is it hard to say no sometimes?

_____
_____
_____

Why does God tell me to be straightforward in my response?

_____
_____
_____
_____

Have you ever been let down by a failed commitment?

_____
_____
_____
_____
_____

Day Six

Fear of Success

When I am afraid, I put my trust in you.
-Psalm 56:3

We've all heard of the fear of failing; but who ever thought that you could be afraid to succeed? As I sat at the circular table in the women's class, I and the others were encouraged to answer the question: *"Are you living out your passion in a consistent way?"* I had to admit that I was about fifty-fifty. Some days I felt ablaze with drive; while others I wondered what the heck I had gotten myself into.

As we went around the table, I discovered that most of the women admitted that they weren't one hundred percent consistent. The girl next to me shocked me with her raw honesty, "the fear of success!" she boldly declared. "If I reach that point, I'm afraid of the pressure of always having to live up to that standard," she confessed.

"Wow!" I thought to myself. She said what most of us were probably feeling, but were too unaware or ashamed to say. I know I have often felt the weight of living up to a standard I have set. I know the self-induced pressure of reaching the next level of success.

Dear daughter of God, we are neither to fear success nor failure. Our God given work is to "believe".

Our hearts must be so sold in trust toward God that we truly believe that we can do all things through Christ. He is your strength, and He will do it. Rest in His promise.

Prayer:

Father, help me to trust in you and not in myself. Give me the courage to dream again. Heal my heart of every disappointment and failure. Let me see my failures as a learning experience. Grow my faith everyday as I meditate on your word. Let me believe again in impossible things. Amen.

Reflections:

How have you been afraid of success?

_____

_____

_____

How has fear affected your trust in God?

_____

_____

_____

How can you overcome your fear?

_____

_____

_____

_____

Day Seven

Blabber Mouth

Like golden apples set in silver is a word spoken at the right time.
-Proverbs 25:11 (ISV)

How wonderful is it that God gave us the power to uplift and encourage each other with our words? Have you ever been feeling down and discouraged, then out of the blue you receive an encouraging call? Or have you ever turned on the radio to hear a song that spoke directly to where you were? Well, that's what God wants us to be for others.

Unfortunately, we have the power to wound people with the lips that were meant to uplift. It has taken me a long time to learn this lesson, and I still miss the mark, but I am learning the art of watching what I say. According to the book of James, the tongue is an unruly evil. "With the tongue we praise our Lord and Father, and with it we curse human beings, who have been made in God's likeness" (James 3:9). Ouch!

As Christian women, we know we are to be kind and love each other with God's love; but life can overwhelm us and we can easily lose our way.

I pray that God would give you a special grace to use your words wisely, and to speak words that will edify those you come into contact with. We never know what another person is going through, so let's be determined to use our mouths as a blessing.

Prayer:

Lord, You said that life and death are in the power of the tongue *(Proverbs 18:21)*. Help me use my mouth to speak life over those You have placed in my care. Make me quick to listen and slow to speak. Show me how to encourage those who come across my path daily, so that I can bring glory to You. Amen.

Reflections:

Recall a time when you said something you shouldn't have.

_____

_____

_____

How did you feel afterwards?

_____

_____

_____

How do you think the other person felt?

_____

_____

_____

Day Eight

Rock Steady

Come," he said. Then Peter got down out of the boat, walked on the water and came toward Jesus. But when he saw the wind, he was afraid and, beginning to sink, cried out, "Lord, save me!"
-Matthew 14:29-30

A wind was brewing, the boat began to rock. Colossal waves rocked the tiny boat back and forth. The disciples were without their teacher and they were afraid. Jesus sent His disciples ahead of Him. He stayed behind to dismiss the large crowd He had miraculously fed hours earlier. In no rush to follow His disciples, Jesus slid away to a mountain alone to pray. Meanwhile, His disciples feared their impending deaths. Where was Jesus now?

However, at just the right time, a mysterious figure came towards them walking on the water. It was Jesus. He reassured them and told them not to be afraid. He even called Peter to Himself, and in a moment unlike any other in all of history, Peter defied the law of physics. He was partaking in a miracle. He too was walking on the water. Yet, in a moment of fear, he began to look at the harsh winds and, becoming afraid, he began to sink.

In times of trouble, we can begin to sink spiritually when we take our eyes off Jesus.

How easy it is to look with our natural eyes and make decisions that we often regret when all we need to do is trust in the gentle leading of our Savior Jesus. May we trust Him always.

Prayer:

Father, help me trust you beyond what my eyes can see. Let my faith be in you alone and not in my circumstances. Give me the courage to step out in faith and not lose heart. Amen.

Reflections:

How have you allowed fear to stop you from pursuing your passion? When?

_____

_____

_____

_____

What's one step you can take toward pursuing your dream today?

_____

_____

_____

_____

Day Nine

The Best Dressed

Your beauty should not come from outward adornment, such as elaborate hairstyles and the wearing of gold jewelry or fine clothes.
-1 Peter 3:3

Have you ever seen a beautiful woman and thought, "I'll bet she has everything"? It's so easy to look at outer appearances and think that all is perfect. Truthfully, the most beautiful people are sometimes the most insecure. I know for myself, the times I feel most self-conscious are when I'm all put together. I have to make sure my makeup doesn't get smudged, keep my nice clothes from getting dirty, and prevent my freshly done locks from getting frizzy. It's a lot of work.

Our culture places a great deal of emphasis on outer beauty; but God doesn't want our primary concern to be our outward appearance. According to the bible, God wants us to concern ourselves with having a beautiful heart; but what does that look like? A beautiful heart is a heart that desires to please God. Instead of seeking the approval of others, God wants us to seek His approval.

Ladies, the best thing we can put on is not diamond earrings or fine clothing, but a heart that longs for God.

Let your desire for Him outweigh every other desire in your life. Let your value come from the love the He has for you.

Prayer:

Lord, I don't want my worth to be measured by my appearance. Show me how to adorn myself with Your love and kindness. Allow others to see the fruit of a peaceful and gentle spirit in my life. Thank You that my worth is not based on my outer appearance. Help me to see others the way You see them and to love others as You love them. Amen.

Reflections:

How has our culture influenced women's perception of beauty?

_____

_____

_____

_____

Do you think the current cultural beauty standards are attainable? Why?

_____

_____

_____

_____

Day Ten

Unshakeable

And the rain fell, and the floods came, and the winds blew and slammed against that house; and yet it did not fall because it had been founded on the rock.
-Luke 6:25

    I can see the scenario playing like an epic Hollywood film. Two neighbors are nestled snugly in their beds; each the proud homeowner of prime beachfront real estate. The summer night sky is calm and clear. It seems as though it is going to be another uneventful night. Then, out of nowhere, thick black consumes the sky. Waves violently crash upon the once peaceful landscape. Harsh winds beat against each house throughout the night.

    As daylight breaks, the damage is undeniable. The house to the left is nothing more than dreams and memories. The house to the right stands as tall as the day it was built, unscathed by its recent ordeal. How could this be?

    In the book of Luke, Jesus explains the tale to his wide eyed disciples. He explains that those who put His teaching into practice are like a wise man who built his house on a rock.

But those who hear His words and don't do them are like a foolish man who built his house upon the sand.

Prayer:

Father, teach me to be as the wise who builds his house on a rock. Show me how to build a solid foundation of trust in You alone. Give me an obedient heart that I might follow You with an undivided heart. Amen.

Reflections:

Why is it important to obey God?

_____

_____

_____

Think of a time you disobeyed God. What was the result?

_____

_____

_____

What will you do differently next time?

_____

_____

_____

_____

Day Eleven

From Craze to Praise

From the end of the earth will I cry unto thee, when my heart is overwhelmed: lead me to the rock that is higher than I.
-Psalm 61:2 (KJV)

In times of pain and suffering, it's all too easy to lose sight of the good things God has for us. Just as Peter took his eyes off Jesus in the midst of the storm, we too can take our eyes off Him. He wants us to come to Him that he might give us His strength.

Too often we lean on our own abilities and put our confidence in what we can do. When things fail we become worried and complain to God for not being with us. According to His word, God will never leave us nor forsake us. We are the ones who end up leaving God in the dust.

If we call upon Him, He promises to answer. He cannot forget us *(Isaiah 49:15)*. He longs to be gracious to us and lavish us with compassion *(Isaiah 30:18)*. We must call out to Him so that He can give us His strength *(Isaiah 41:10)*.

Prayer:

God, I confess my need for You every moment, every day and every hour. Show me how to rest securely in Your love. Teach me to be anxious for nothing. Help me to trust You at all times. Amen.

Reflections:

What causes your heart to become overwhelmed?
_____
_____
_____
_____

What is the solution for a heavy heart?
_____
_____
_____
_____

What is the result of turning to God for help?
_____
_____
_____
_____

Day Twelve

Are You Gonna Eat That?

Therefore, whatever you want others to do for you, do also the same for them.
-Matthew 7:12 (HCSB)

For me, being pregnant and hungry is akin to a hunting lioness. If you interrupt me or get in my way, the results will not be pretty. I was tired. I barely had enough energy to lift a finger; much less think of cooking breakfast for anybody else.

With all the strength I had, I pulled myself into the kitchen and managed to whip up a delicious veggie and cheese omelette with crispy homemade hash browns on the side; a meal fit for a queen. I smiled as I gazed upon my wonderful creation anticipating the experience to come; eating. As I was about to leave the kitchen, I heard a still and quiet voice clearly say, "I want you to give that food to your husband."

"What! Why in the world would I do such a thing?", I reasoned to myself. "He's not pregnant. He can get off the couch and fix his own meal. Do you know how long it took me to make this food? Do you know how tired I am right now?"

When I finished rant, I decided to listen to that still small voice and give the beautiful food I had made for myself to my husband.

Obeying God is so much better than getting our way. After eating, my husband confessed how much that food blessed him. I could tell he really needed that - not the food so much as the act of kindness.

Prayer:

Lord, help me to treat others the same way I want them to treat me. Show me how to give the best I have to offer even when I'm tired, weary and even disappointed. Help me to love others the way you love them. Amen.

Reflections:

Why is it challenging to put others first?

_____
_____
_____
_____
_____

Remember a time you did a good deed for another. How did the person feel? Did they say anything?

_____
_____
_____
_____
_____
_____
_____

Day Thirteen

Relax, it's Just a Test

Jesus, full of the Holy Spirit, left the Jordan and was led by the Spirit into the wilderness
-Luke 4:1

After Jesus was baptized by John the Baptist, the clouds parted and a voice from heaven proudly proclaimed, "This is My Son with Whom I am well pleased!". After this miraculous event, the bible records that Jesus was lead to the desert to be tempted by the devil for forty days.

After forty days without food, Jesus was hungry. The enemy tempted Jesus with food, power, and questioning God. Jesus overcame every temptation with God's word. The devil couldn't get Jesus to sin. Jesus knew His purpose. He knew who He was.

Being tempted is not a sin. Giving in to that temptation is what brings sin. God promises us in 1 Corinthians 10:13, that no temptation is too great for us to overcome. He says that He will help us and give us the strength to endure it.

Remember, Jesus was tempted too. God knows that when we overcome temptation it makes us stronger, so don't sweat temptation. Remember, it's just a test that you can pass with flying colors.

Prayer:

Father, I thank You for being present with me in the midst of temptation. Thank You for Your grace to endure and to overcome it with the power of Your word. Thank You for loving me. In Jesus' name. Amen.

Reflection:

Why was Jesus lead into the wilderness?

_____

_____

_____

What temptations did Jesus face?

_____

_____

_____

_____

How did Jesus overcome temptation?

_____

_____

_____

_____

Day Fourteen

Quit Lying!

Therefore each of you must put off falsehood and speak truthfully to your neighbor, for we are all members of one body.
-Ephesians 4:25

Is it okay to tell little white lies? I mean, we know God says to tell the truth, but what can a tiny little white lie hurt? Everybody does it, right? According to 1 Corinthians 5:6, "a little leaven leavens the whole lump". In other words, something that starts out small grows over time. Small lies turn into medium-sized lies, which turn into full grown lies. Women, don't deceive yourselves. A lie is a lie.

An example of a small lie is telling someone that you're a stoplight away when you're really five lights away. They may believe you at first, but when you take longer than they think you should, they will realize you weren't telling the truth.

Another problem with lying is motives. Why do we lie? Do we lie to protect others, or to keep people happy? The times I have lied are usually when I wanted to avoid facing unwanted consequences.

Prayer:

Father, help me to see lying the way You do. You say in Your word to speak the truth to one another. Help me to do this even when I will suffer consequences. Create in me a clean heart that I might please you. Amen.

Reflections:

Think of one white lie that you've told?

___

Why do we view white lies as acceptable?

___

Day Fifteen

Grudges Come Easy

Bear with each other and forgive one another if any of you has a grievance against someone. Forgive as the Lord forgave you.
-Colossians 3:13

  You want me to do what? Sometimes forgiveness seems impossible to do; but, thankfully, what's impossible with man is possible with God. Forgiveness doesn't mean excusing another person's abuse. One of the best descriptions of forgiveness that I have ever heard is, "forgiveness is setting a prisoner free and realizing that the prisoner was you."

  Pain is real. Hurt is real. Offences are real. It's not a sin to be offended when someone hurts or mistreats us. The issue is when, instead of confronting that person and making peace, we quietly hold resentment against them.

  Daughter of God, if you're holding onto unforgiveness, I challenge you to set yourself free. They don't deserve it, you say? No, but neither did we when Christ, the innocent, died for the guilty. In God's eyes, all sin is the same. No sin is greater than the other. So save yourself some stress, heartache, and suffering, and simply forgive.

Prayer:

Father, help me to forgive everyone that has ever hurt me, abused me, or mistreated me. Heal my heart of all distrust so that I can build healthy relationships. Let me not make others pay for the mistakes of others. I give You my heart and I forgive now. Amen.

Reflections:

How does unforgiveness affect our attitude?

_____
_____
_____

How can unforgiveness affect our ability to build healthy relationships?

_____
_____
_____
_____

What people in your life do you need to forgive?

_____
_____
_____
_____

Day Sixteen

Ain't Nobody Got Time For That

A person's wisdom yields patience; it is to one's glory to overlook an offense.
-Proverbs 19:11

    I have been offended by many people on different occasions. However, in defense of the other party, they probably didn't even realize it. Most people have not acquired the art of using wisdom when they speak. They end up blurting out the first thing that comes to their minds, and as a consequence, end up offending others.

    If we are honest with ourselves, we can admit that we too are guilty. In a moment of anger, we lost patience. Or while conversing with a girlfriend, we allowed ourselves to speak negatively about others. We have all done it. We are all guilty. It's a beautiful thing when we can forgive others for the same shortcomings we also possess.

Prayer:

Father, give me a thick skin. Help me to overlook the offenses of others. Give me wisdom and understanding so as not to offend others. Amen

Reflections:

Why is it "a glory" for us to overlook an offense?

_____
_____
_____

How do you feel when you are offended?

_____
_____
_____

Can you remember a time when you offended someone?

_____
_____
_____
_____
_____

Day Seventeen

A Fool is as a Fool Does

Do not answer a fool according to his folly, or you yourself will be just like him.
-Proverbs 26:4

Has someone ever said something to you so ridiculous you didn't even bother to answer him? I know this has happened to me. Most times I just smile and walk away. This is not always easy. The bible says that offenses will come. It's how we handle those offenses that make us wise or foolish, according to the bible.

Based on God's word, being a fool is determined by our action; not our knowledge. How we behave is the defining factor. I know we've all seen the wino on the street talking to himself and saying all kinds of crazy things. People usually do one of two things: ignore him, or make fun of him.

If not careful, we can look just as foolish by arguing with others. It's better to disagree with someone and move on. I've seen grown people get into fights over the smallest of remarks. It's not worth it. Be wise and walk away.

Prayer:

Father, give me the grace and self-control to walk away instead of arguing. Help me to be patient with others in spite of their shortcomings. Help me to control my mouth when I want to lash out in anger. Teach me to honor You in my speech! Amen.

Reflections:

What happens to you when you respond to a fool?

_____

_____

_____

_____

How can you prevent yourself from being tempted to answer a fool?

_____

_____

_____

_____

Day Eighteen

Weakness Is the Greatest Strength

But he said to me, "My grace is sufficient for you, for my power is made perfect in weakness." Therefore I will boast all the more gladly about my weaknesses, so that Christ's power may rest on me.
-2 Corinthians 12:9

    I don't like the feeling of not being able to do something. I enjoy being able to work and accomplish a task on my own without help from anyone. When I have trouble finishing something, I admit I get a little frustrated. In our culture, asking for help can be seen as a sign of weakness. Doing something solo brings a sense of victory and comes with its own bragging rights.

    Although it feels great to do things on our own, God made it so that we need each other. The thought of exposing our weakness can seem humiliating, but it's in discovering this truth we find true liberation. Being a one woman army is exhausting. We want people to think that we have it all together. Honey! No one has it together; no matter how good they look on the outside.

Allow yourself to be vulnerable. It's actually a strength that too few possess. Realize that depending on God is necessary. So if you're feeling overwhelmed, confess your weakness to Christ and allow him to make you strong.

Prayer:

Lord, I thank you that when I am weak I am strong. Help me to confess my weakness to you daily. Help me not be afraid to ask for help from others when I need it. Give me a humble heart. Amen.

Reflections:

How does confessing our weakness to God give us strength?

_____
_____
_____

What are some areas you need help in?

_____
_____
_____

What's hindering you from reaching out?

_____
_____
_____

How will reaching out help you?

_____
_____
_____

Day Nineteen

Seeing Isn't Believing

For we live by believing and not by seeing.
-2 Corinthian 5:7 (NLT)

If we have to see something to believe it, we don't have faith. When Jesus walked on the earth, He performed many miracles. Yet those who witnessed them still asked for more signs in order to believe. Jesus said, "Blessed are those who have not seen, and have yet believed" (John 20:29).

As women who confess faith in Christ, we are to live by faith. Although we will never be perfect, we must continually seek to see through the eyes of faith. We won't always get it right, but that's why there's grace.

Take your eyes off your circumstances. God is not limited by the things we are. Your situation, your finances, and your past don't intimidate Him. He is the same yesterday, today and forever. Hallelujah!

Prayer:

Thank you, Lord, for being bigger than my circumstances. Forgive me for the times I have put my faith in what I could see instead of in You. Today I put my trust in You alone. Amen.

Reflections:

What does it look like to walk by faith?

_____
_____
_____
_____
_____

What's one practical way you can trust God today?

_____
_____
_____
_____
_____
_____
_____
_____

Day Twenty

Believe & It Will Come

Now faith is confidence in what we hope for and assurance about what we do not see.
-Hebrews 11:1

Did you know that everyone has faith? Some utilize it to acquire wealth opportunities and live an amazing life; while others speak negative things into their own lives. It's called the Law of Attraction. It was Solomon who once said, "there's nothing new under the sun" *(Ecclesiastes 1:9)*.

How is it that people who don't even believe God exists use His word to gain success? The fact of the matter is that God's word works wherever it's put into practice. Christian or not. There's no magic prayer or formula. Jesus said, believe and receive. Ask and it will be given; knock and the door will be opened *(Matthew 7:7)*.

What do you need to believe in God for today? It may seem impossible, but God promises that He will never leave nor forsake us *(Hebrews 13:5)*. Close your eyes and visualize what you want! See yourself reaching that goal, starting that business, marrying that godly man. He will do it. He promises He will.

Prayer:

Father, thank You for giving me faith. Help me to keep my eyes on You so that I might walk in Your peace *(Isaiah 26:3)*. Help me to set aside time daily to meditate on Your word. I need You. Amen.

Reflections:

What's one goal or dream you have?

What obstacles are standing in your way?

Visualize every obstacle being removed?

Day Twenty-One
Your Gift Will Make Room

A man's gift makes room for him and brings him before the great.
-Proverbs 18:6

      I recently watched a documentary about young entrepreneurs. One man was the youngest person to receive a million dollar funding for an idea he had. From his youth, this boy was in love with computers. Another young lady loved developing web pages for her friends. By the time she was fifteen, she had over one hundred monthly customers and was making an impressive five figure income. Later on, she developed a software program to help small businesses manage their finances.

      She was able to raise $50,000 for her first startup company, and today her company is worth millions of dollars. The bible says that our gifts will make room for us and bring us before the great. A gift will give you access money cannot buy. No matter what your gift, decide to use it to glorify God. Don't worry about the journey, just begin with one step at a time.

Prayer:

Thank You, Father, for the gifts that You have given me. Give me the courage to use them for Your glory. Help me to trust in You and not in my own abilities. Help me to remain humble. Amen.

Reflections:

What gifts do you posses?

_____

_____

_____

_____

How can you use them to bless others?

_____

_____

_____

_____

_____

Day Twenty-Two

A Wise Tongue

She opens her mouth with wisdom, and the teaching of kindness is on her tongue.
-Proverbs 31:26 (ESV)

If we're not careful, our words can cause damage to those we love. As a mother, I find it's sometimes easy for me to lose patience with my children when I'm tired. Little things that I can usually ignore begin to irritate me. A small request can seem unreasonable and cause me to wound the little hearts in my care.

Being careful with our tongue is a skill that we must all acquire if we want to have healthy relationships. The damage done to relationships by speaking recklessly can last for a lifetime.

We must work at being thoughtful of the feelings of others. We will make mistakes, but that's what grace and forgiveness are for. Let's strive not to take others for granted.

Prayer:

Father, You said life and death are in the power of the tongue (Proverbs 18:21). Help me to use me mouth to bring life and not death, healing and not destruction. Let the law of kindness be on my tongue at all times. Amen.

Reflections:

Why is it important to choose your words carefully?

_____

_____

_____

What happens when you don't?

_____

_____

_____

How do you feel when someone says something they shouldn't have?

_____

_____

_____

_____

Day Twenty-Three

Wise Time

Look carefully then how you walk, not as unwise but as wise, making the best use of the time, because the days are evil.
-Ephesians 5:15-16

Why does it always seem as though there's never enough time in a day. If I'm honest, when I have a full plate, my personal time with God often gets put on the back burner. When we neglect the most needful thing, it shows. Remember when Jesus was a guest in the house of Mary and Martha? Martha was desperately concerned with cleaning and meal preparation. Mary was concerned about just one thing: Jesus.

In the midst of our daily lives, raising children, tending to our marriages, and working a nine to five (like Martha) we can forget what's most important: our relationship with Christ.

As we return to our first love, we will find that we maneuver through life with a lot more ease. Let's seek first His kingdom and receive grace for today.

Prayer:

Thank You for today. Help me to make You number one in my life. Forgive me for putting other things before You. You said without You I can do nothing (John 15:5). I need You. Give me strength for today. Amen.

Reflections:

Why does God tell us to seek the kingdom first?

_____

_____

_____

How is your day when you don't put God first?

_____

_____

_____

What hinders you from putting God first in your life?

_____

_____

_____

Day Twenty-Four

What Have You Been Eating?

But I discipline my body and keep it under control, lest after preaching to others I myself should be disqualified.
-1 Corinthians 9:27 (ESV)

No matter how hard you try, you can't hide it. And as I attempted to maneuver my way into my favorite pair of jeans, the truth was abundantly clear. I had to ask myself, "What have you been eating?" When people with food allergies eat certain types of foods, they break out in hives and get blotches and rashes on their skin.

One way I know I've eaten too much chocolate is the appearance of pimples on my face. What we eat shows. Whether it's in the form of glowing skin and healthy hair or acne and tight fitting clothing. We can't hide it. Similarly, what we eat spiritually cannot be hidden. Have you ever caught yourself behaving in a way that even surprises you? If you dig a little, you will probably discover that you didn't spend time reading and meditating on God's word.

Just as evident is when we take the time to sit and spend that personal time with our Savior. We are more patient, understanding and forgiving towards others. Ladies, watch what you eat! What goes in will come out. Ladies, watch what you eat! What goes in will come out.

Prayer:

Father, help me to be wise in what I expose myself to. Help me to honor You in the things I listen to on the radio, the shows I watch on television and even the company that I keep. Give me wisdom in all things. Amen.

Reflections:

Have you had a healthy spiritual diet lately?

_____

_____

_____

_____

What are some areas that you need to work on?

_____

_____

_____

_____

_____

Day Twenty-Five

All I Need

So if we have enough food and clothing, let us be content.
-1 Timothy 6:8 (NLT)

From television advertisements to our favorite music videos, our culture is always telling us we need more. Although, I would say I'm pretty financially sensible, when I see women rocking a Michael Kors purse I get a little envious. It's the status associated with it that makes me want it because, honestly, I don't think MK purses are all that cute. It's the price tag that screams, "I've arrived" that has women of all races, ages, and income levels at MK stores.

If we are to become women of virtue, we must place our value on the things that God does. No, there is nothing wrong with wanting or owning expensive things. There is something wrong if our motive for buying those things is to fit in and and feel important. Our value must come from God alone.

In the book of Matthew, we are told to seek first His kingdom and all these things will given to us as well. God promised not to withhold any good thing from those who seek Him *(Psalm 84:11)*.

Hallelujah! So let's put our focus back in the right place and be content with Christ.

Prayer:

Father, thank You for providing for my daily needs. I confess that You are good. Help me to be grateful for the things that I have. Rid me of every insecurity that makes me want things to feel accepted. Lord, You accept me; and that's good enough. Amen.

Reflections:

Why is it important to be content?

_____

_____

_____

What happens to us when we are not content?

_____

_____

_____

How do insecurities affect our behavior?

_____

_____

_____

_____

Day Twenty-Six

Beaches & Bikinis

Then you will know the truth, and the truth will set you free.
-John 8:32

The sun was ablaze, the breeze gentle and my family and I were ready to enjoy a rare day in the state of Washington: eighty degree weather in April. We unloaded our clan and proceeded to find a spot on the beach. When we got there, a man with his two little girls was leaving just in time to open up the perfect spot for our family of six.

As I sat down, my eyes casually scanned the beach to view my fellow beach goers. My heart sank as I spotted two gorgeous, thin, tanned, thong-wearing twenty-something's not too far from me. At the time, I was five months pregnant. Moments before, I was feeling pretty cute. But the sight of these two girls began to make me feel a bit insecure. Sad to say, I let that day be ruined by my own insecurities.

Reflecting back, I can now see the truth. No person, man or woman can diminish my worth. Another woman's beauty doesn't deflect mine. God calls me the apple of His eye *(Prov. 17:8)*. I am beautiful. I am unique. I am a Queen!

Don't allow lies and insecurities to discourage you. You are beautiful, smart and talented; perfect just the way God made you. Rejoice in this truth and be set free today!

Prayer:

Lord, help me to see the beauty in me. Let me not feel threatened by the gifts and beauty of others. Heal me of all wounds of rejection and insecurity. Let my confidence and my security be in You alone. In Jesus' name. Amen.

Reflections:

How does the truth set us free?

_____

_____

_____

Why do we need to be free?

_____

_____

_____

Imagine yourself free from all insecurity and shame. What does it look like?

_____

_____

How does it feel?

_____

_____

Day Twenty-Seven

Theft

No weapon forged against you will prevail, and you will refute every tongue that accuses you. This is the heritage of the servants of the LORD, and this is their vindication from me," declares the LORD.
-Isaiah 54:17

Insufficient funds. "How could this be?" I thought. I've always been meticulous about managing my money; so I knew something wasn't right. I called to check my recent transactions, and there it was - a purchase that I know I didn't make, from a place I've never heard of. Was I angry? Surprisingly, no! I was in "take care of it" mode.

It was evening, so I had to wait until the next morning to take care of it. As I explained to the lady in the bank, I had misplaced my card a few weeks earlier. Instead of getting a new card number, I asked them to send me another one. I didn't want to have to memorize another card number. I had that card for over a decade.

In the end, I got all my money back. No weapon of the enemy (frustration, anger, or blaming) was able to take root in my life. Glory to God!

Prayer:

Lord, help me to trust You in every situation and circumstance. When things come into my life to upset me, show me how to rejoice in Your Word. Show me how to completely trust in You. Amen.

Reflections:

What situations in your life look unfavorable?

_____

_____

_____

_____

What can you do in the midst of these circumstances?

_____

_____

_____

Why does God tell us to "cast all our care" on him?
(1 Peter 5:7)

_____

_____

_____

_____

Day Twenty-Eight

Flattery

Whoever rebukes a person will in the end gain favor rather than one who has a flattering tongue.
-Proverbs 28:23

It's something we all want to hear. The sound of it makes our cheeks blush and our ego's expand: flattery. The scary thing about flattery is that it's deceitful and misleading. According to the Merriam-Webster dictionary, flattery is, "praise that is not sincere". Flattery can cause us to see ourselves in a way that is false and unrealistic.

People who flatter have ill motives. If we allow ourselves to be moved by it, we can be deceived. God tells us to judge ourselves with sober judgment *(Romans 12:3)*. Flattery intoxicates us so that we cannot clearly judge our own state.

Allow your security and accolades to come from God. Let us not be like the Pharisees who loved the praise of man more than the approval of God *(John 12:43)*.

Prayer:

Open my eyes that I may discern a true compliment from flattery. Let my heart not be deceived by the insincere applause of others. Let my desire be to receive applause from You alone. Amen.

Reflections:

Can you tell the difference between a compliment and flattery?

_____

_____

_____

What is the difference?

_____

_____

_____

Why do people use flattery?

_____

_____

_____

What does flattery do to the recipient?

_____

Day Twenty-Nine

He is God

He says, "Be still, and know that I am God; I will be exalted among the nations, I will be exalted in the earth."
-Psalm 46:10

It was the most trying time in my life. All of a sudden I was a single mom, and I was homeless. I had become used to the abuse, belittlement and daily bashing; it was my normal. I did what I had to do to cope. He threatened to take my kids away if I ever left. At this point, I was isolated. My children were all I had.

Through a series of events beyond my control, we ended up at a women's shelter. It was a difficult time. I was completing my bachelors degree, trying to figure out childcare arrangements and dealing with emotional trauma. I can't tell you how I kept it together. It was only God who kept me.

His grace is enough. His love is enough; if we just take the time to see it. It was hard at times, but, as I stood still in the glory of His presence, I found He gave me peace. Today, God has blessed me with a true man of God. We serve together and raise our beautiful family together. His grace is sufficient. Be still and know that He is God. He will right every wrong.

Prayer:

God, I thank You that You see all things. Thank You for saving me, watching over me and protecting me. Each day let me not lose sight of Your goodness. Let me take time each day to be still in Your presence. Give me strength in tough circumstances. Amen.

Reflections:

What circumstances do you need God's strength in today?

_____

_____

_____

_____

How does being still in God's presence help us to overcome?

_____

_____

_____

_____

_____

_____

Day Thirty

You Got This!

I can do all this through him who gives me strength.
-Philippians 4:13

It was the first day of my Master's program. I was so nervous. I had no idea what to expect. I dropped out of high school on the first day. I was a minority. I was a single parent. I felt so out of place; yet I pushed through my fears and walked into the prestigious classroom filled with hopeful teachers.

Pursuing a Master's Degree was one of the most rewarding things I've ever done. I worked hard. I stayed up late. I cried. I sacrificed and I prayed, a lot! I met some wonderful people and had experiences that I will never forget. As I look back, I can't help but smile remembering all the times I wanted to give up. Each time, God found a way to encourage me and, through His grace, I kept pushing on.

On June 12, 2012, I graduated from the Master's in Teaching Program, my friends and family applauding me. I dropped out of high school the first day, so this was a big deal for me. I did it! And no one can ever take that away from me.

God's word is true. His promises are faithful. He will never fail you or let you down. Simply, believe. Trust and pray. You can do all things because He gives you strength. Rejoice! Celebrate His grace, for He is good!

Prayer:

Father, help me to stand on all Your promises. I need You. Help me to stand on Your word that says nothing is impossible *(Matthew 19:26)*. Thank You for being with me. I love you. Amen.

Reflections:

What seems impossible in your life right now?

_____

_____

_____

_____

What obstacles stand in your way?

_____

_____

_____

How has God promised to help you?

_____

_____

_____

_____

About the Author

Krystle Laughter is an author, life coach, recording artist, and public speaker. She has been interviewed and heard on National radio stations and appeared on the popular Trinity Broadcasting Network. She was born and raised in Washington and is the youngest of six children. She enjoys writing, singing & utilizing her creative talents. She holds an A.A, B.A., & M.I.T. She lives with her hubby and their four beautiful children. Krystle and her husband are expecting their fifth child this summer.

www.krystlelaughter.com

To learn more about Krystle follow her on all social media outlets:

FACEBOOK: authorkrystlelaughter
YOUTUBE: Krystle Laughter
INSTAGRAM :@krystlelaughter
TWITTER: laughterkrystle

Many women are living lives far less than they deserve, all because they never learned how to love themselves. Loving yourself first is the secret to healing, creating healthy relationships, and becoming a confident woman because you teach others how to treat you. If you've ever done love wrong, married or single, this book is for you. Buy one for yourself & gift another to a friend!

THE AFTER **ABUSE** SERIES

The *After Abuses Series* was designed to help survivors of domestic violence overcome the effects of abuse through self-empowerment & healing. Written by an abuse survivor, this series speaks to the obstacles survivors face & equips them with knowledge, tools, & encouragement to help them move forward. Coming Soon!

Losing someone you love is painful. It's important to remember the good memories you shared. *When I Think of You* follows a little girl as she experiences the joy of remembering a loved one. This book is the perfect gift for children and adults alike to help them remember the happy moments that makes us smile. Meditate on the good times in *When I Think of You*. Order your copy today!

Made in United States
North Haven, CT
27 February 2023